SCHOLASTIC
News
Nonfiction Readers®

Our Earth
Clean Energy

by Peggy Hock

Children's Press®
An Imprint of Scholastic Inc.
New York Toronto London Auckland Sydney
Mexico City New Delhi Hong Kong
Danbury, Connecticut

These content vocabulary word builders are for grades 1–2.

Content Adviser: Zoe Chafe, Research Associate, Worldwatch Institute, Washington, DC

Reading Consultant: Cecilia Minden-Cupp, PhD, Early Literacy Consultant and Author, Chapel Hill, North Carolina

Photographs © 2009: age fotostock/Tom Grill: 5 top left, 10; Alamy Images: 1, 9 (Steve Allen Travel Photography), 23 bottom right (M Stock), 5 top right, 8 right (Pablo Paul), back cover, 5 bottom left, 17 (Steven Poe), 23 top left (Jim West); Corbis Images/Walter Geiersperger: 23 bottom left; Getty Images: front cover (Dave King), 21 bottom (Panoramic Images), 7 (Baerbel Schmidt); NASA/Nick Galante/Dryden Flight Research Center Photo Collection: 19; National Geographic Image Collection: 21 top (John Eastcott and Yva Momatiuk), 21 center (Norbert Rosing); Photo Researchers, NY/Science Source: 4 bottom right, 18; PhotoEdit/Dana White: 23 top right; Superstock, Inc.: 4 bottom left, 8 left (age fotostock), 15 (Anton Vengo), 2, 20 bottom; VEER: 20 top (Corbis Photography), 4 top, 11 (Henryk T. Kaiser), 5 bottom right, 13 (ML Sinibaldi).

Book Design: Simonsays Design!
Book Production: The Design Lab

Library of Congress Cataloging-in-Publication Data
Hock, Peggy, 1948–
Clean energy / By Peggy Hock.
    p. cm.—(Scholastic news nonfiction readers)
Includes bibliographical references and index.
ISBN-13: 978-0-531-13833-5 (lib. bdg.) 978-0-531-20433-7 (pbk.)
ISBN-10: 0-531-13833-X (lib. bdg.) 0-531-20433-2 (pbk.)
1. Renewable energy sources—Juvenile literature. 2. Fossil
fuels—Environmental aspects—Juvenile literature. I. Title. II.
Series.
TJ808.2.H63 2008
333.79'4—dc22   2007051896

CONTENTS

WORD HUNT

Look for these words as you read. They will be in **bold**.

dam
(dam)

pollution
(puh-**loo**-shuhn)

scientists
(**sye**-uhn-tists)

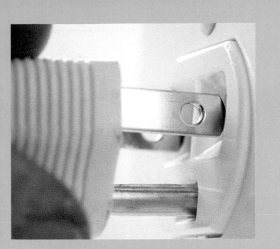

electricity
(ih-lek-**tris**-uh-tee)

oil
(oyl)

solar panels
(**soh**-lur **pa**-nuhlz)

turbines
(**tur**-binez)

Your Energy

How do you use energy?

You need energy to keep your house bright and cozy.

You need energy to run your computer or TV.

People get energy from different places.

It takes energy to cook food and clean up. How many things in this picture use energy?

Getting energy can make **pollution**.

For example, burning **oil** for energy makes air pollution.

There are cleaner ways to get energy. Energy can come from water, wind, and sunshine.

pollution　　**oil**

This moving water has a lot of energy. The energy can be turned into energy that you can use.

People turn energy from water into **electricity**.

First they build a **dam** to hold back water in a river.

Gates on the dam open to let the water flow.

The water moves through special machines that turn its energy into electricity.

electricity

dam

Water moving through Hoover Dam makes electricity for millions of people.

Wind energy is another kind of clean energy.

Wind turns giant fans called wind **turbines**.

The turbines help turn wind energy into electricity.

turbines

This wind farm produces electricity for a nearby city.

You can get hot standing in the sun.

What you feel is the sun's energy at work.

Energy from the sun is another kind of clean energy.

Energy from the sun can melt ice cream!

People use **solar panels** to collect the sun's energy.

The panels turn the energy into heat or electricity.

Then the heat can be used to warm buildings and swimming pools.

The electricity can power lights, TVs, and computers.

The black rectangles on this roof are solar panels. They help heat the house and keep the pool warm.

Clean energy can cost a lot.

Scientists are looking for ways to make it cost less. They are also trying to make it easier to use.

Then more people can use clean energy. That will be good for all of us!

scientists

Solar planes like this one are being tested by scientists.

Five Places to Get Clean Energy

1

Wind: Energy from the wind can be made into electricity.

2

Sun: Energy from the sun can become electricity or heat.

5

Waves: People are learning how to turn energy from waves into electricity.

4

Heat: People can use heat energy from deep inside Earth.

3

Water: Energy from moving water makes electricity for many people.

YOUR NEW WORDS

dam (dam) a wall on a river to hold back water

electricity (ih-lek-**tris**-uh-tee) a form of energy used to power lights, TVs, and other devices

oil (oyl) a thick liquid found underground used to make gasoline and other fuels

pollution (puh-**loo**-shuhn) harmful materials that damage Earth's air, water, or soil

scientists (**sye**-uhn-tists) people who study nature and the world around us

solar panels (**soh**-lur **pa**-nuhlz) devices that collect energy from the sun and turn it into heat or electricity

turbines (**tur**-binez) engines that produce electricity when rotated by wind, water, or steam

THE SUN'S ENERGY AT WORK

Solar stoplight

Solar car

Solar house

Solar light

INDEX

FIND OUT MORE

Book:

Petersen, Christine. *Alternative Energy.* New York: Children's Press, 2004.

Website:

Energy Information Administration: Energy Kid's Page
http://www.eia.doe.gov/kids

MEET THE AUTHOR

Peggy Hock lives near San Francisco, California. She likes to go backpacking with her husband and two grown children. She drives a hybrid car, one that is powered by gasoline and electricity.